This CyberSecurity Book

Belongs to

Introduction to Cybersecurity for Teens

The Internet can be a scary place. The Internet that keeps evolving and rapidly becoming the main way of interacting with the Real World.

Staying **safe online** can be really overwhelming — most of us have our photos, personal communications, credit cards, financial information, and devices exposed to threats every single day without even knowing that they're in danger.

But Fear Not!

The vast majority of cyber attacks can be easily prevented with the proper tools, some basic education, and plain old common sense.

This Activity Book will show you the most common Online Threats, how to Prevent them and how to be **Safe Online**, so you can **Protect Yourself** and your **Family**.

Most Common Online Threats

 Malware: Software designed to damage a computer, steal data, or financially exploit unsuspecting users. Common malware types include ransomware, trojans, and spyware.

 SCAMS: A fraudulent scheme to deceive users into giving away their personal information and money, using emails, text messages, websites, social media accounts, and online dating profiles.

 Identity Theft: Using another person's personal information (e.g. name, social security number, credit card, etc.) without permission.

 Data Breaches: The release of personal information (such as email addresses, usernames, passwords, and even credit card numbers and social security numbers) to the general public and dark web servers. Companies with your Data can get Hacked and can make it available online or for sale.

Cyber Crossword

Across

[1] Software that is secretly installed on a device without the knowledge of the owner.

[5] Software or hardware that tracks keystrokes and keyboard events.

[7] Is malware that employs encryption to hold a victim's information at ransom.

[10] A program that appears to be useful but has hidden malicious functions.

Down

[2] An individual, group, organization, or government that executes an attack.

[3] A weakness in the device security that makes it open to attacks.

[4] An unexpected and small defect, fault, flaw, or imperfection in a program or device.

[6] Malicious software that is designed to make unwanted changes to settings or software, to cause errors in software or on devices, or to spy on personal information.

[8] A fake website pretending to be another legitimate website.

[9] A self-replicating, self-propagating, self-contained program that uses networking mechanisms to spread itself.

Solution

```
              ¹S  P  Y  W  ²A  R  E
                              T
                              T
        ³V                    A
         U                    C
         L              ⁴B    K
         N              U     E
        ⁵K  E  Y  L  O  G  G  E  R
    ⁶M        R
 ⁷R  A  N  ⁸S  O  M  W  A  R  E
    L     P              B
    W     O              I
    A     O              L
    R     F              I     ⁹W
    E     I           ¹⁰T  R  O  J  A  N
          N              Y     R
          G                    M
```

Across

[1] Software that is secretly installed on a device without the knowledge of the owner.

[5] Software or hardware that tracks keystrokes and keyboard events.

[7] Is malware that employs encryption to hold a victim's information at ransom.

[10] A program that appears to be useful but has hidden malicious functions.

Down

[2] An individual, group, organization, or government that executes an attack.

[3] A weakness in the device security that makes it open to attacks.

[4] An unexpected and small defect, fault, flaw, or imperfection in a program or device.

[6] Malicious software that is designed to make unwanted changes to settings or software, to cause errors in software or on devices, or to spy on personal information.

[8] A fake website pretending to be another legitimate website.

[9] A self-replicating, self-propagating, self-contained program that uses networking mechanisms to spread itself.

Cyber WordSearch

```
G T W O R M E N U A X I F T O H R E B G
K R K W O X I K E Y L O G G E R G P V W
V O P I Z E Q Y S U U P Z N U A E B G Y
K J G O R J M H W Q Y G M P N E R P L B
J A L Y R E X H H C V V D O M R A V P I
G N Y A U B K V L Z H A S G Q A W Q S Q
G G C X M C Q C Q U T C I Y R W L U I P
J K C Z Y P W V A E R M D U Y Y A S J R
Q M P K T A F G S T U H E J E P M S R B
S T V A I T K S L V T B W V X S D Q A H
I U D R L C P A Q J G A X K K I M V N E
R X V P I H Z Q O I N F U P D J J R S L
S P W B B I J L E A I H H J B T M M O M
W P V H A N Y K O T F E S V E M R V M E
F U G B R G Y R J U O E A I E T P X W T
Q E B C E B O E S Z O Q H W D Y C F A H
I Z N B N U T D W T P Y E Q G K D G R P
I P Y L L G K B O M S Q U G L I F B E Q
L X J J U T R Y P X P U Q C N F D Q N S
P U S R V P G T P I H I S E R K Z G T U
```

ATTACKER	BUG	MALWARE	KEYLOGGER
SPOOFING	SPYWARE	TROJAN	VULNERABILITY
WORM	RANSOMWARE	UPDATES	PATCHING
HOTFIX			

Most Common Malware

Virus: A malicious program that repeatedly causes your computer to crash.

Trojan: Pretends to be a legitimate file to gain unauthorized access to your device in order to steal data, install other malware, or give hackers remote access to your computer.

Spyware: Allows hackers to quite literally spy on your computer and track your browsing history online.

Adware: Clutters your desktop with pop-up ads, inserts unwanted results in your search bar, and even redirects your browser while you're online.

Cyber Maze

Find your way to a fully Updated Device

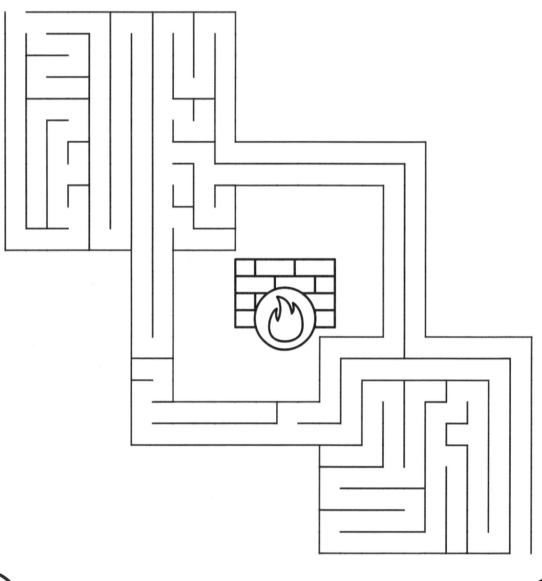

Cyber Crossword

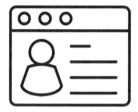

Across

[3] A data breach is an incident where information is stolen or taken from a system without the knowledge or authorization of the system's owner.

[5] A relatively minor release or version upgrade to an existing Application that adds minor features, corrects bugs or improves security.

[7] A correction or removal of an anomaly or "bug" in an existing Software or App Major's Release.

[9] Relating to or involving the application of biological data to assist in the authentication process.

[11] A package of one or more files used to address a problem in a software product.

[12] a software tool designed to take advantage of a flaw in a computer system, typically for malicious purposes such as installing malware.

Down

[1] is the hidden collective of internet sites only accessible by a specialized web browser. It is used for keeping internet activity anonymous and private

[2] irrelevant or unsolicited messages sent over the internet, typically to a large number of users, for the purposes of advertising, phishing, spreading malware, etc.

[4] Multi-factor authentication secondary method of authentication in which a user is granted to access to a website or application after a successful Password Login.

[6] a process or set of rules to be followed in calculations or other problem-solving operations, especially by a computer.

[8] Identity theft committed through a malicious link contained within a text message or SMS

[10] An application, especially as downloaded by a Mobile device.

Solution

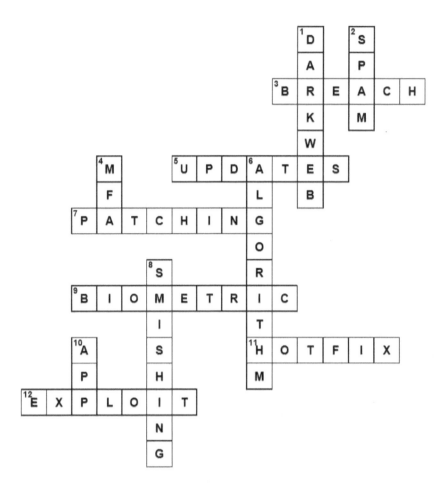

Across

[3] A data breach is an incident where information is stolen or taken from a system without the knowledge or authorization of the system's owner.

[5] A relatively minor release or version upgrade to an existing Application that adds minor features, corrects bugs or improves security.

[7] A correction or removal of an anomaly or "bug" in an existing Software or App Major's Release.

[9] Relating to or involving the application of biological data to assist in the authentication process.

[11] A package of one or more files used to address a problem in a software product.

[12] a software tool designed to take advantage of a flaw in a computer system, typically for malicious purposes such as installing malware.

Down

[1] is the hidden collective of internet sites only accessible by a specialized web browser. It is used for keeping internet activity anonymous and private

[2] irrelevant or unsolicited messages sent over the internet, typically to a large number of users, for the purposes of advertising, phishing, spreading malware, etc.

[4] Multi-factor authentication secondary method of authentication in which a user is granted to access to a website or application after a successful Password Login.

[6] a process or set of rules to be followed in calculations or other problem-solving operations, especially by a computer.

[8] Identity theft committed through a malicious link contained within a text message or SMS

[10] An application, especially as downloaded by

Cyber WordSearch

```
B W J J C K S W Z B R G R I N P B Y G D
F W T V C N N J Q S A A B E I K O O C E
Z N O Y I C L J Y M W P H Z Y Y U A S D
H Z N I C H R C W I Y P P W I A V D J K
R K V O T A P M C S G K C Z R D C W V W
N U P Y I E F P U H X W Y O X A A A C E
C H Y S B T T B X I J V O R P R D R I S
M B U Z T N A C T N O T H Z Z K X E R V
L C C H H H N C G G K T V A M W Y Z T W
C E P B F Q L D I I S N F C A E M E E O
G Z M H D K W P T L U B U H S B O Y M Q
T O G Q J R D K T F P V W Z R P S F O M
B K E Y L O G G I N G P H Q Z W A R I H
L Y L H C A E R B J U L A F C B J M B T
U G X N Y A M K V M J C P G L J V F K I
G I O O F A A I N D I T N C H X G S Y R
C C T M R U X B P C N M C L Q Z Y D X O
V E W R M L A N D I K X K E T A J F K G
L J K Z C D D S F I P Q W P J A Y Z Q L
H Z X T I O L P X E R V V S W G B T U A
```

SMISHING	BREACH	DARKWEB	ALGORITHM
MFA	BIOMETRIC	SPAM	EXPLOIT
APP	APPLICATION	KEYLOGGING	COOKIE
ADWARE	ROOTKIT		

Most Common Malware

 Ransomware: Encrypts and locks your device unless you pay a ransom to recover your account.

 Rootkit: Gains extremely deep access to your system, allowing it to hide from antivirus scanners and make changes to the operating system and other essential components.

 Fleeceware: is a type of malware mobile application that come with hidden, excessive subscription fees.

 Cryptojacker: Uses your computer as part of a larger network to mine cryptocurrency. This can put a ton of strain on your computer, causing slowdown, crashing,

 Worm: A self-replicating, self-propagating, self-contained program that uses networking mechanisms to spread itself.

Cyber Maze

Find your way to a fully Updated Device

Cyber Crossword

Across

[3] is a type of malware mobile application that come with hidden, excessive subscription fees.

[4] software that automatically displays or downloads advertising material such as banners or pop-ups when a user is online.

[6] Spyware is a term that is used to describe software that is to secretly gather information about a user's activity.

[9] the use of a computer program to record every keystroke made by a computer user, especially in order to gain fraudulent access to passwords and other confidential information.

[11] is a type of cybercrime that involves the unauthorized use of people's devices (computers, smartphones, tablets, or even servers) by cybercriminals to mine for cryptocurrency.

[12] a program or piece of software designed to fulfil a particular purpose.

Down

[1] a packet of data sent by a web server to a browser, which is returned by the browser each time it subsequently accesses the same server, used to identify the user or track their access to the server.

[2] the use of a computer program to record every keystroke made by a computer user, especially in order to gain fraudulent access to passwords and other confidential information.

[5] a set of software tools that enable an unauthorized user to gain control of a computer system without being detected.

[7] Cybercriminals use this by creating false web pages or emails that are designed to look trustworthy to get personal information from people.

[8] Internet term used to describe junk email, bulk email, pop-ups, or communication that is unasked for.

[10] A fraudulent business scheme too good to be true.

Solution

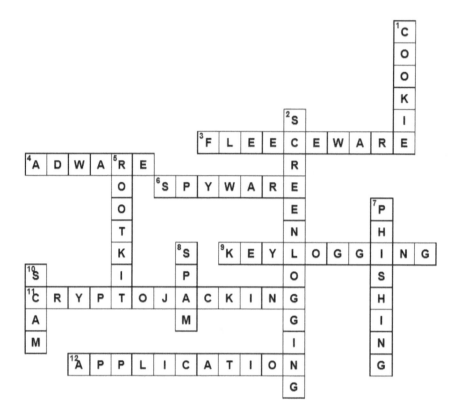

Crossword grid solution:

- **1 Down:** COOKIE
- **2 Down:** SCREEN (S-C-R-E-E-N-I-N-G reading: SCREENING)
- **3 Across:** FLEECEWARE
- **4 Across:** ADWARE
- **5 Down:** ROOTKIT
- **6 Across:** SPYWARE
- **7 Down:** PHISHING
- **8 Down:** SPAM
- **9 Across:** KEYLOGGING
- **10 Down:** SCAM
- **11 Across:** CRYPTOJACKING
- **12 Across:** APPLICATION

Across

[3] is a type of malware mobile application that come with hidden, excessive subscription fees.

[4] software that automatically displays or downloads advertising material such as banners or pop-ups when a user is online.

[6] Spyware is a term that is used to describe software that is to secretly gather information about a user's activity.

[9] the use of a computer program to record every keystroke made by a computer user, especially in order to gain fraudulent access to passwords and other confidential information.

[11] is a type of cybercrime that involves the unauthorized use of people's devices (computers, smartphones, tablets, or even servers) by cybercriminals to mine for cryptocurrency.

[12] a program or piece of software designed to fulfil a particular purpose.

Down

[1] a packet of data sent by a web server to a browser, which is returned by the browser each time it subsequently accesses the same server, used to identify the user or track their access to the server.

[2] the use of a computer program to record every keystroke made by a computer user, especially in order to gain fraudulent access to passwords and other confidential information.

[5] a set of software tools that enable an unauthorized user to gain control of a computer system without being detected.

[7] Cybercriminals use this by creating false web pages or emails that are designed to look trustworthy to get personal information from people.

[8] Internet term used to describe junk email, bulk email, pop-ups, or communication that is unasked for.

[10] A fraudulent business scheme too good to be true.

Cyber WordSearch

```
O G A H A Z A C B B A B T M E R Q S W U
T S I L E T I H W T I T P K M R G H K V
M C R I H X P F H S S H J H Z V N N B R
P D O Z T E R A W Y P S I T N A I G P N
A F R E V R E S N E U Y M P O A N H M A
M L G M F S A E V P S X L G R H I B J D
V Z E V A W Y Q R V E M J C N D M R E X
X M Y R J U V Q U A I N T Z G M A O T D
M H E Q T V T F L O W R T P T P T W Y C
E J S F F G O H C X A E U I Z I A S A J
Z H S P A M N D E C T P C S Y X D E B G
P Y S F T S C I X N C L M E R N U R K B
R B E N M S V T R G T C O P E R K Y K Y
A U K P R L I O O O M I H G X L R S O R
A Y M Q C F H L H C T I C R E L F J N F
T X T H J L Y A V A S I Z A F F V U F X
N U M Y T Y B Y B H D Q N B T X B L E C
H S P Y W A R E I L U G L O V I F L I X
L S Y S T Z L N P U E P N X M Q O L V M
K N Q B E F G B R T K M A C S M K N U Y
```

FLEECEWARE	PHISHING	SPAM	SCAM
SPYWARE	VIRUS	DATAMINING	SERVER
WHITELIST	ANTISPYWARE	ALERT	AUTHENTICATION
MONITORING	BROWSER		

Safety Tips Against Malware

 Don't Download email attachments from people you don't know.

 Don't Download files from untrustworthy websites directly or using Torrent sites or Programs.

 Install a reputable Antivirus program on your Devices, schedule periodical Scans and keep it up to date.

 Don't Connect USB Drives or Storage Devices you don't know their origin. These can contain Malware that is executed the minute it's plugged in to your Device.

 Keep your Devices Updated and Patched. So new Vulnerabilities and Bugs are addressed.

Cyber Maze

Find your way to a fully Updated Device

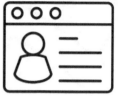

Cyber Crossword

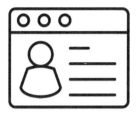

Across

[3] A list of websites that are considered trustworthy and are granted access or privileges.

[6] A list of entities that are blocked or denied privileges or access.

[7] It is a computer program that is designed by a cybercriminal to steal information, modify or damage data, or send or display false messages.

[8] A program that specializes in detecting and blocking or removing forms of spyware.

[9] The process or techniques used to analyze large sets of existing information to discover patterns.

[11] A computer that provides data to other computers, typically over the internet or a network.

Down

[1] The process of verifying the identity or other attributes of a person or device.

[2] Is a software program used to navigate the world wide web.

[4] Observing activities of users and devices.

[5] Systems and programs that live on the internet.

[10] A notification of a specific attack or threat that needs to be looked at.

Solution

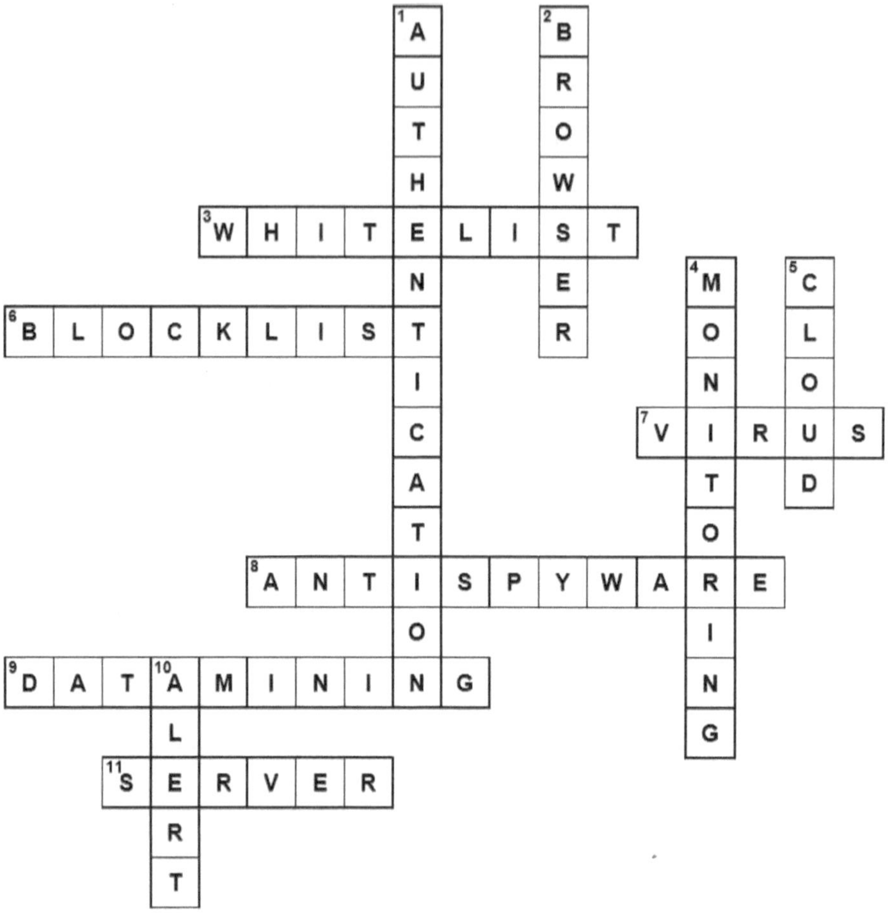
1 AUTHENTICATION
2 BROWSER
3 WHITELIST
4 MONITORING
5 CLOUD
6 BLOCKLIST
7 VIRUS
8 ANTISPYWARE
9 DATAMINING
10 ALERT
11 SERVER

Across

[3] A list of websites that are considered trustworthy and are granted access or privileges.

[6] A list of entities that are blocked or denied privileges or access.

[7] It is a computer program that is designed by a cybercriminal to steal information, modify or damage data, or send or display false messages.

[8] A program that specializes in detecting and blocking or removing forms of spyware.

[9] The process or techniques used to analyze large sets of existing information to discover patterns.

[11] A computer that provides data to other computers, typically over the internet or a network.

Down

[1] The process of verifying the identity or other attributes of a person or device.

[2] Is a software program used to navigate the world wide web.

[4] Observing activities of users and devices.

[5] Systems and programs that live on the internet.

[10] A notification of a specific attack or threat that needs to be looked at.

Cyber WordSearch

```
K U C Y B E R C R I M E P V Y R V I Q S
A U K N I L R E P Y H S B B Y T N X G Y
S A O W U I Z S Y F T D D W X E T S O H
X I D E X C S O N D E E G H M U D V A G
W A Z U Z F Y C N B B D N T X D I C L P
Z V Y D O P R Z O U C H Y P L E K U T O
P D S Y R L P M G M Q K R P I E H M H E
A C H U A Y C G P M M E W G R O E B H C
S O K K N M I F O T F A M Z P K K B Y L
S O K R X N K J T O G X N A P G R T L V
W K U R G M O W Z U H A T D N H R G M Z
O I O N S M T P U V H T R L N R H L A G
R E C T A N T I V I R U S X B H E E R W
D S I G J W X C J D G G M P R Y K S Q V
Y L G O C P O E H M A R G O R P U F U F
Z Z F D T K B M V V Y Z K Z H E D A V F
V X M S E J C Y B E R S E C U R I T Y U
G R L X L G N J N L N I E C C I S E Z U
G U B C U W E B J M A U A J B K X E Q M
W J R K Z J L K I U E A R X R M I N Q T
```

CLOUD	COMMAND	DEBUGGING	PROGRAM
ANTIVIRUS	PASSWORD	USERNAME	HACKER
COOKIE	CYBERCRIME	CYBERSECURITY	HYPERLINK

Most Common Scams

 Gaming Scams: Criminals pose as interested gaming partners on gaming lobbies, websites or social media, be mindful with the people you play online with, specially if they ask for personal information.

 Lottery and Charity Scams: Hackers appear to represent legitimate charities, lotteries, or sweepstakes and then convince seniors that they have won a contest or persuade them to make a donation.

 Tech Support Scams: Criminals claim to be tech support and flag a fake computer or mobile device issue. They offer to solve the problem by using a program to take over a device to gain personal information.

 Relative Impersonation Scam: Criminals pose as a relative who ask for financial assistance. Seniors are mostly targets of this type of scam.

 Government Impersonation Scams: Criminals claim to be government employees and demand payment or personal information regarding taxes, social security, pensions, etc.

Cyber Maze

Find your way to a fully Updated Device

Cyber Crossword

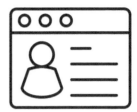

Across

[4] A word, phrase, or string of characters that a user keeps secret and uses to log into a program.

[6] Protective measures and practices designed to protect networks, devices, programs, and data from attack by cybercriminals.

[10] The act of stealing, corrupting, or viewing of other people's personal or private information or data.

[11] Software program or hardware device that filters data entering and leaving a computer, device, or network.

[13] A program is an application, or a piece of software. It is written in code, also known as programming language.

Down

[1] Program that protects your computer or network against computer viruses, or malware.

[2] An image, rotation of images, or animation that replaces the desktop or display when after a period of no use or interaction.

[3] The process of finding and fixing bugs in a computer program.

[5] An icon, graphic, photo, or text, that links to another page or file.

[7] An unauthorized user who attempts to or gains access to an information system.

[8] An instruction given to a computer, by a user, that tells it to do something.

[9] A name that was chosen for identification to log into a program.

[12] Small text file that is stored on your computer from a website. Websites use cookies to track data and recognize preferences.

Solution

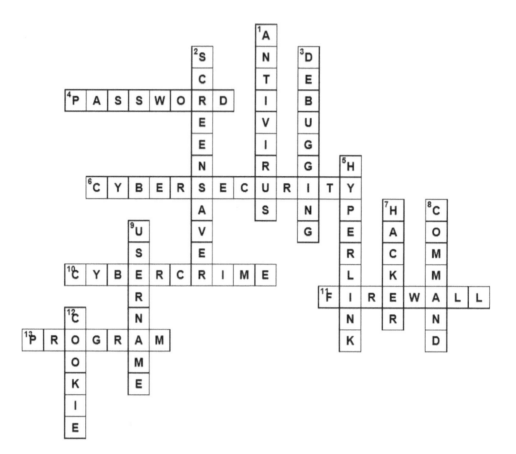

The crossword solution contains the following filled answers:

Across:
- [4] PASSWORD
- [6] CYBERSECURITY
- [10] CYBERCRIME
- [11] FIREWALL
- [13] PROGRAM

Down:
- [1] ANTIVIRUS
- [2] SCREENSAVER
- [3] DEBUGGING
- [5] HYPERLINK
- [7] HACKER
- [8] COMMAND
- [9] USERNAME
- [12] COOKIE

Across

[4] A word, phrase, or string of characters that a user keeps secret and uses to log into a program.

[6] Protective measures and practices designed to protect networks, devices, programs, and data from attack by cybercriminals.

[10] The act of stealing, corrupting, or viewing of other people's personal or private information or data.

[11] Software program or hardware device that filters data entering and leaving a computer, device, or network.

[13] A program is an application, or a piece of software. It is written in code, also known as programming language.

Down

[1] Program that protects your computer or network against computer viruses, or malware.

[2] An image, rotation of images, or animation that replaces the desktop or display when after a period of no use or interaction.

[3] The process of finding and fixing bugs in a computer program.

[5] An icon, graphic, photo, or text, that links to another page or file.

[7] An unauthorized user who attempts to or gains access to an information system.

[8] An instruction given to a computer, by a user, that tells it to do something.

[9] A name that was chosen for identification to log into a program.

[12] Small text file that is stored on your computer from a website. Websites use cookies

Cyber WordSearch

```
E N M W T S E R A W D R A H Y S X S K Y
L W V K S O D X H H X T I Y N J W J U R
T K Y Y O E C P O J Q L K C Y F M A H Y
X A J C Y J S A L E Y Y B E J D U F T Q
X F L O P E E A Z E P N K O S T D D M D
G I N R I H R Z B W I E A N Z I Y B L G
B N M B C X E R W A O I R Y P U K C A B
P C S P A L E R I O T O S S N E X M B N
Q S Q X E I M P E S R A Q X O P Z A S E
T T O L E R Y M R T K O D X B N N X X M
X A I B L K S Z W G U N S P L D A E B L
M O E D C A S O G D R P J S W F X L N F
A B V R O D W X N V D G M I E D G D Q A
A I R I H Y P E L A G Z D O D C F D C W
E I R Y Q T N O R T T T X X C Q O N O K
Z N O Z X B V I W I H E E V M T S R Y A
D G M X O X D C S T F R P I X E L K P N
Y B M V R A D Q N R S T P S R S R G N W
B F Q C F Z Q E S G M M Z N K M F U F S
U P O N W D Z E U M J J Y R A A U R X B
```

FIREWALL	IMPERSONATE	BACKUP	BANDWIDTH
DATABASE	THREAT	HARDWARE	HTML
IP	PIXEL	PROCESSOR	PERSONAL
COMPUTER			

Safety Tips Against SCAMS

 **Don't click on links and don't Download anything**: If you're even slightly suspicious about the communications you're receiving, don't follow any links or download any files.

 **Go to the Source**: Google the charity, lottery, tech department, or even government office potentially being impersonated. You can contact these organizations via phone or email and verify if you're being contacted by a scammer or a real person.

 **Ask Clarifying Questions**: Ask yourself, "Why would a tech support person need you to download a file? Or, "How did you win a something that you never entered in the first place?" By asking yourself or someone you trust these types of questions, it will likely expose whether the message is from a legitimate source or not.

 **Don't Reply or Engage:** If it doesn't feel right, it probably isn't. Don't reply or continue the conversation after you have talked to someone you trust about it or found out the source is legitimate.

Cyber Maze

Find your way to a fully Updated Device

Cyber Crossword

Across

[3] Refers to different sets of instructions, or programs, for a computer to follow.

[4] Copy of a file or resource that can be accessed if the original gets lost or destroyed.

[5] Stands for personal computer.

[7] Pretending to be someone else online.

[8] A collection of data that is organized in a way that makes it easy for someone to access the information inside in various ways.

[10] A network Address, or Internet Protocol Address.

[12] An indicating of potential danger or harm.

Down

[1] An icon that resides on a computer's desktop and links to a specific program or file.

[2] Is used to describe all of the physical components that make up a computer.

[5] The part of a computer that processes and carries out the instructions a user gives it.

[6] Measure of how much data you can move through an Internet connection in a given amount of time.

[9] A tiny area of illumination on a computer's monitor.

[11] Hypertext Markup Language, he language used for creating Web pages.

Solution

SHORTCUT
HARDWARE
SOFTWARE
BACKUP
PC
PROCESSOR
BANDWIDTH
IMPERSONATE
DATABASE
PIXEL
IP
HTML
THREAT

Across

[3] Refers to different sets of instructions, or programs, for a computer to follow.

[4] Copy of a file or resource that can be accessed if the original gets lost or destroyed.

[5] Stands for personal computer.

[7] Pretending to be someone else online.

[8] A collection of data that is organized in a way that makes it easy for someone to access the information inside in various ways.

[10] A network Address, or Internet Protocol Address.

[12] An indicating of potential danger or harm.

Down

[1] An icon that resides on a computer's desktop and links to a specific program or file.

[2] Is used to describe all of the physical components that make up a computer.

[5] The part of a computer that processes and carries out the instructions a user gives it.

[6] Measure of how much data you can move through an Internet connection in a given amount of time.

[9] A tiny area of illumination on a computer's monitor.

[11] Hypertext Markup Language, he language used for creating Web pages.

Cyber WordSearch

```
Y D V H K K E Y W X W L Y N M J D A O O
R P Y E K I L O B Y T E X R L S C S T E
O F O T W F Y P J L E D A S X I E O D L
M J D Y K G B A F F S J C C A E F U T S
E V B B G I Z C K Z N Y O W T N F F T J
M I I A N G M K I C U R X W E W P O U D
V M Q G G A H E D E E A W Z R X T C F
N O U E V B A T K C N K Y X N O K D T O
L T X M L Y Q S R Z A J Q L M T S U R B
K H D R E T T W E B Y S B O D I F L O U
E E R I I E H Q R S M I J L H N S S H N
K R K E C F P M Y F W V H X Q O P T S D
K B Z N P T S L P O C M Q V M M U R K A
E O X D S A S B Y Q H Z J W I O K T I O
Y A M G Q T P K V M E R A W T F O S J N
B R O Y L C B L R Y I L V W V F H A Z L
O D T A D D N O L M F L G H O R W X Y A
A O Z M L W O F O A X S B A I F A V D P
R V F N M U W K N Z W K L C Q Y Z I Q S
D S Q W O O K L F C R C C F C C I T Q P
```

SOFTWARE	SHORTCUT	WALLPAPER	DATA
KILOBYTE	MEGABYTE	GIGABYTE	MEMORY
PACKETS	MOTHERBOARD	KEYBOARD	MONITOR

Identity Theft Techniques

 Phishing: Phishing is the act of creating fake websites, phone numbers, or email addresses that mimic legitimate sources for the purpose of getting information, stealing money, or deploying malicious programs on user devices.

 Smishing: Phishing messages are sent via email, social media, or text message. These messages may inform you that you have money waiting for you, ask you to fill out a survey, or may even trick you into reimbursing a government or financial institution.

 Social Engineering: Is a manipulation technique that exploits human error to gain private information, access, or valuables. In cybercrime, these "human hacking" scams tend to lure unsuspecting users into exposing data or giving access to restricted systems. Attacks can happen online, in-person, and via other interactions.

 Shoulder Surfing or Spying: Can occur anytime you use your PIN or password to access your personal accounts in public. Places such as the ATMs or Internet Cafes, where the identity thief can see the screen or lets you use a compromised Device that may contain keylogging or screen logging software.

Cyber Maze

Find your way to a fully Updated Device

Cyber Crossword

Across

[3] or KB, is 1,024 bytes.

[5] A video display terminal or output device.

[6] or GB is 1,024 megabytes.

[7] A circuit board holds many of the important parts of the computer hardware and allows communication between them.

[9] The instructions, program, or operating information that tells a computer what to do, or how to perform a task.

[11] A packet is a small amount of data that includes information on where it is coming from, where it is going to.

Down

[1] Physical device that stores information for operating systems, software and programs, and hardware.

[2] Wallpaper is also known as the background on a desktop. It is usually a picture or digital image that was chosen by the user.

[4] Information that has been stored on a computer.

[5] or MB, is 1,024 kilobytes.

[8] Input device made up of buttons that reference letters, numbers, and symbols.

[10] External hardware output device that prints copies of documents from a computer to a piece **of paper.**

Solution

Across

[3] or KB, is 1,024 bytes.

[5] A video display terminal or output device.

[6] or GB is 1,024 megabytes.

[7] A circuit board holds many of the important parts of the computer hardware and allows communication between them.

[9] The instructions, program, or operating information that tells a computer what to do, or how to perform a task.

[11] A packet is a small amount of data that includes information on where it is coming from, where it is going to.

Down

[1] Physical device that stores information for operating systems, software and programs, and hardware.

[2] Wallpaper is also known as the background on a desktop. It is usually a picture or digital image that was chosen by the user.

[4] Information that has been stored on a computer.

[5] or MB, is 1,024 kilobytes.

[8] Input device made up of buttons that reference letters, numbers, and symbols.

[10] External hardware output device that prints copies of documents from a computer to a piece

Cyber WordSearch

```
U L D V H I D X N J N A U O I Y M G I W
Y R A J Z N V R Y X C T I K R Y Z X M Y
S S O J W T B I T Q V B C T J H S X A E
G F L Y I E R Q S P E A K E R S J B H K
C W P B B R S C P P R O D P T L S O S G
R S U N O N L J R L W I V A G L M I N N
W N J W O E K V B Z V N S Q O E Y M L L
K J E D K T T F Z J A M N O T L L P V L
X U C N M S H C I Z Z L F H A N K S D
D I Q W A C D E C K R O W T E N T W J S
O G O O R A W R W Q V M L K X Y P N O W
Z U M W K N X L E S A Z C M R E D U K D
E V K E S N R Y X T M U D O X D R F E W
G I I B Y E M K M V N J E U U A O T K W
E C G C T R X V B W A I E S L A W C F L
T N W G H U R E K J X I R E L R Y W K N
L Q I D N A L F E M A I L P Q K E P A C
Q V S L R N X Q S J V J T G Q L K D H I
O J A M N X O Y X W A X H S O A D W T B
U Y A B A O E H E T I S B E W O D K A W
```

MOUSE   PRINTER   SCANNER   SPEAKERS

DOWNLOAD   EMAIL   INTERNET   NETWORK

ONLINE   UPLOAD   BOOKMARKS   KEYWORD

WEBSITE

Tips Against Identity Theft

Don't Click on Unknown links: Phishing messages and smishing messages frequently contain links that can lead you to unsafe sites.

Check the email address and not the sender name: It's really easy to deceive someone with a fake sender name when sending emails. When this happens, the sender name may be familiar, but the email address doesn't match the sender name. If you see emails from companies or people you know, make sure the email address matches the name of the company or known sender. Scam emails use machine generated email addresses such as "njqk.22yfx8@2djfjycg.us". If the email was actually from the company, the email address would be from "@companyname.com".

Look for Typos: Phishing attacks frequently use similar spellings as the brands they are trying to spoof, for example "amazn.com", or "support@micr0soft.com" to fool users.

Go to the Source: Use Google to look up the organization being imitated on Google, and compare the legitimate website to the potential phishing site. or go to their website directly.

Cyber Word Scramble

1. WREATPYINSA _____

2. OLCUD _____

3. ELART _____

4. RSVIU _____

5. NPV _____

6. BEDUGGIGN _____

7. TCOUTSHR _____

8. EIKBYOTL _____

9. DAAT _____

10. WITBSEE _____

11. HIDWNABDT _____

12. OPRCOERSS _____

13. OMCNAMD _____

14. CP _____

15. AZDHRA _____

16. HTML _____

17. COOKIE _____

18. UGB _____

19. ESPTACK _____

20. REAWHADR _____

Cyber Crossword

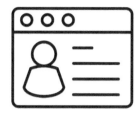

Across

[4] A form of online harassment that may include posting hurtful or inappropriate things about another person, or sending unwanted emails or instant messages.

[8] Data being sent from a computer or device to the internet.

[10] To uncover or reveal text to plain text by means of a cryptographic system.

[11] The sharing of data through a collection of computers, servers and devices.

Down

[1] A website, or site, is a group of web pages that are related to a homepage.

[2] Is a global network that provides information and communication.

[3] The network of information technology infrastructures, that includes the Internet, networks and computer systems.

[5] Sometimes called a "favorite," saves a web page's address.

[6] A user, computer, or device that is currently connected to the internet, or a network.

[7] Word or group of words that are used to help a person, and a search engine, find a page or information.

[9] Stands for Virtual Private Network.

[10] To convert encoded text to plain text by means of a code.

Solution

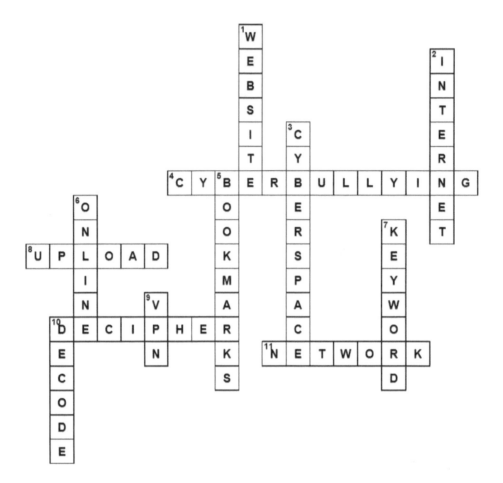

The crossword solution:

- **1 Down:** WEBSITE
- **2 Down:** INTERNET
- **3 Down:** CYBERSPACE
- **4 Across:** CYBERBULLYING
- **5 Down:** BOOKMARKS
- **6 Down:** ONLINE
- **7 Down:** KEYWORD
- **8 Across:** UPLOAD
- **9 Down:** VPN
- **10 Across:** DECIPHER
- **10 Down:** DECODE
- **11 Across:** NETWORK

Across

[4] A form of online harassment that may include posting hurtful or inappropriate things about another person, or sending unwanted emails or instant messages.

[8] Data being sent from a computer or device to the internet.

[10] To uncover or reveal text to plain text by means of a cryptographic system.

[11] The sharing of data through a collection of computers, servers and devices.

Down

[1] A website, or site, is a group of web pages that are related to a homepage.

[2] Is a global network that provides information and communication.

[3] The network of information technology infrastructures, that includes the Internet, networks and computer systems.

[5] Sometimes called a "favorite," saves a web page's address.

[6] A user, computer, or device that is currently connected to the internet, or a network.

[7] Word or group of words that are used to help a person, and a search engine, find a page or information.

[9] Stands for Virtual Private Network.

Cyber WordSearch

```
P M Y J E C N E U Q E S N O C O P Y S E
G N I Y L L U B R E B Y C O U D T C T B
Y L D E C I P H E R L L A R L C P A F S
C U S V S J C E D Q F U H K H Y Y V T P
S C M H R R B J R W R V N A V W R I B Z
Z Y S L I I H Q I R J M N O Z D C R Z C
R B O C I T K U X V B D S J D W N P X S
S E K S G D X M M G Q F R E E N E I B Y
B R Q S I X T R G Z X Y C F X S D K C V
O S G Y L S L R Q A R R L Z F Z B O Y R
F P S Z W P Y O W Y Y E Z W B D C Q S H
D A W O W N S B D P D L Z I E Z Z X A S
X C X N B V K V T O D V I D Y R C S N L
Z E S D V S X I C G H K N H S Y H E R W
S Z G B W X O E F L Q E A B V I S S S H
F J B R B N D Z L K V Z V H N V P N N S
K P S V G R P V T H A N M G L H O Q T U
T X E T N I A L P R T R K K J O K I K T
N I P S G X B W D S W F A C M R T T K E
D U M W B D I S R U P T I O N D Y V H T
```

CYBERBULLYING	VPN	CONSEQUENCE	CYBERSPACE
DECIPHER	DECODE	DECRYPTION	DISRUPTION
ENCRYPT	HASHING	HAZARD	PLAINTEXT
PRIVACY			

Tips for when your Identity has been Compromised

 **Notify your Bank**: Your bank will immediately freeze your accounts, preventing any further losses, and it will also begin the process of reimbursement for the funds stolen from your account.

 **Run an antivirus Scan**: It will detect and remove any surveillance malware from your device that could be used to steal future financial information and prolong the identity theft attack. Make sure you're using a reputable antivirus program. Do not Use or Download one offered to you by Ads or Pop-Ups.

 **Change your passwords**: Once your system is free of malware, create strong Passwords for all email, banks and Social Media Accounts. complex Phrases work better than simple word Passwords.

 **Track Payments and Records**: Login to your bank after your new passwords have been set and look at recent transaction records and set up transaction alerts with your bank. This will help register when transactions are made.

 **Talk to your Tech Contact to Report the Breach**: This could be a family member, friend or even support from the vendor who provided the Device or Service.

Cyber Word Scramble

1. RWEKDOY _____

2. BYGTEMAE _____

3. EBGLUYLRICYBN _____

4. CYCESBREAP _____

5. YEMRCIECBR _____

6. ASHGNIH _____

7. OUSTTHRC _____

8. CANERSN _____

9. DASBTAAE _____

10. NMNTAIDIAG _____

11. ANUBLYTIVIREL _____

12. AENUMERS _____

13. ILTEXPANT _____

14. EENUCESQCNO _____

15. ANOJTR _____

16. EPAYRWS _____

17. OENINL _____

18. HNPIRYLEK _____

19. UPBCAK _____

20. ALRELFIW _____

Cyber Crossword

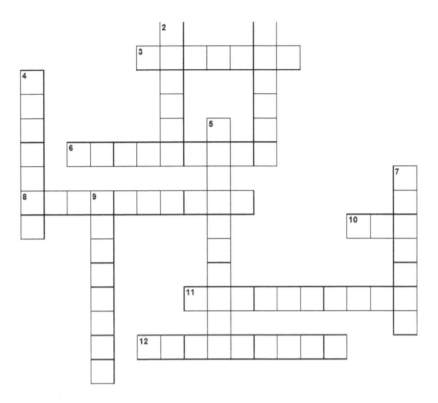

Across

[3] Making sure certain information about the user is safe and protected.

[6] Unencrypted information.

[8] Is malware that employs encryption to hold a victim's information at ransom.

[10] Short Message service is a system for sending short text messages over mobile networks.

[11] An event which causes interruption in operations.

[12] A recognizable, distinguishing pattern.

Down

[1] The generic term encompassing encipher and encode.

[2] A program that appears to be useful but has hidden malicious functions.

[4] Software that is secretly installed on a device without the knowledge of the owner.

[5] The process of transforming ciphertext into its original plaintext.

[7] A process of applying math against a set of data to produce a numeric value.

[9] A fake website pretending to be another legitimate website.

Solution

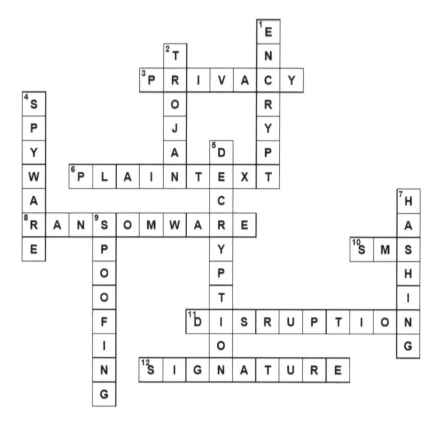

Across

[3] Making sure certain information about the user is safe and protected.

[6] Unencrypted information.

[8] Is malware that employs encryption to hold a victim's information at ransom.

[10] Short Message service is a system for sending short text messages over mobile networks.

[11] An event which causes interruption in operations.

[12] A recognizable, distinguishing pattern.

Down

[1] The generic term encompassing encipher and encode.

[2] A program that appears to be useful but has hidden malicious functions.

[4] Software that is secretly installed on a device without the knowledge of the owner.

[5] The process of transforming ciphertext into its original plaintext.

[7] A process of applying math against a set of data to produce a numeric value.

[9] A fake website pretending to be another legitimate website.

Tips Against Data Breach

 Use unique Passwords: If you have a different password for each of your online accounts, then a data breach won't result in a devastating privacy violation. If you have the same password for most of your accounts, hackers can use that password for multiple sites to gain access to your accounts.

 Change your Passwords Regularly: Many breaches go unreported for months before being found, so it's smart to be proactive and constantly change your passwords. You can use a Password Log or a Password Manager from a reputable source.

 Two-factor Authentication (2FA): (Also Called Multifactor Authentication) A required second step to log into an account after entering your password. This could be a temporary one-time password, a code or notification sent to your phone or a USB token.

 Don't Share your Passwords: Don't share Password or Keys with others that might not observe the same level of safety.

 Protect your Devices: Keep a close eye on your mobile devices. Protect your Devices with Passwords or Passcodes. Never leave your mobile devices unattended.

Cyber Word Scramble

1. EHOAUTNTTANICI _____
2. YOEGELRKG _____
3. AETACKTR _____
4. ESVRER _____
5. IPNOSDTURI _____
6. PMSA _____
7. WSRFTAOE _____
8. MSCA _____
9. ILKCBOTLS _____
10. LOODWNAD _____
11. TOGIRONIMN _____
12. DKEAROBY _____
13. OTARPNESIME _____
14. WRLAEPLPA _____
15. FETWARSO _____
16. BTEAGGYI _____
17. AREHCK _____
18. ASPDRSOW _____
19. YCERNPT _____
20. PCEIRDEH _____

Cyber Maze

Find your way to a fully Updated Device

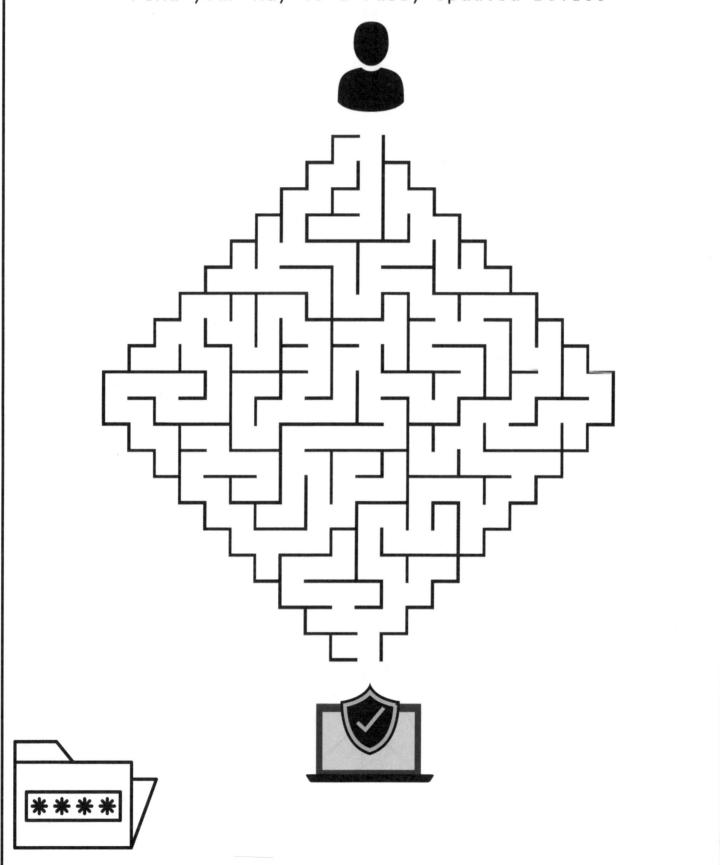

Cyber WordSearch

```
O N L I N E T F S K V Y J H K S N V A Z
O E B G W K P M E J B B S W K L D M T H
P N X Q K T H B I P U V N V P Y G X A X
T N J G V H M M Y S Z S I E A N F T L H
F A V O R I T E Z K T D D X Q E H D Q B
D W H Z X A S L O N E E V S T T I M N G
P N J I I Z J K U O D I M E K T E R A V
A D W S Q Z I O G Y Y S D C B O O E H N
S J X P I C C A T O O L S U Q G X G P V
S L Y T M C M N L J B S Z R F R I A K Z
W U A W A E Q U Y Z G K Y I H O N N C D
O E B P D E T P Y R C N E T D F W A F W
R G K W T O O R X U V X K Y M I W M Q Y
D M C S K O O B J O O E R O T S P P A A
S G U F I W P T T E W H L V K J M F T U
B A I X R E S O L U T I O N L X F C R O
T O Z E W I N D O W S A Z B Y W D D J Y
Q J V S T L U A V P B W X H W T C L U Z
E H P W B Z K D E L B A K A E R B N U U
K Y L L A U T R I V S A W F I M O G Z N
```

MANAGER	TOOLS	VIRTUALLY	UNBREAKABLE
PASSWORDS	ACCOUNTS	ONLINE	APPSTORE
ENCRYPTED	VAULTS	FORGOTTEN	FAVORITE
VIDEOGAME	LAPTOP	WINDOWS	RESOLUTION
SECURITY			

General Online Safety Tips

 <u>Make Social Media Private</u>: Make your Social Accounts as Private as possible and don't share personal information as posts or part of your profile.
Specially if this information can be used to guess your Passwords or Recover Questions.

 <u>Don't Connect your Devices to Public Wi-Fi</u>: When possible don't connect to Public Unknown Wi-Fi networks that could be compromised and/or sniffing network traffic.

 <u>Don't click on ads:</u> If you see a nice deal on a third-party website, don't click on the deal. Instead, go directly to the company's website to ensure that the offer is legitimate.

 <u>Consider Using a VPN Service</u>: If your devices are exposed to Public Networks most of the time, consider a VPN service that can encrypt the traffic coming from/to your Devices.

 <u>Use common sense and be critical</u>: If it's too good to be true, it probably is. Before you download a file or click on a link, consider if the website or source is trustworthy.

Cyber Word Scramble

1. IISURNAVT _____

2. ADMRBRHOTEO _____

3. BRROEWS _____

4. EXPLI _____

5. REENNTTI _____

6. TNCRDEYPIO _____

7. RMOW _____

8. UERRBYSTECCIY _____

9. OINPOFGS _____

10. RSRCASNEVEE _____

11. RKSASPEE _____

12. WTLIIHSET _____

13. RHTATE _____

14. YVPRIAC _____

15. IEAML _____

16. GHNISIHP _____

17. LDOAUP _____

TRUST YOUR INSTINCTS

In the end, **use your common sense** and **trust your Instincts**. If something seems too good to be true, it probably is.

Be nice and respectful to people online but always be wary and if anything seems suspicious, remember that you don't have to take any actions under pressure and make sure you report it or talk to your parents to give you a second opinion.

Remember to Share these Safety Tips with Family and Friends.

Safety is Everyone's Job.

Thank you!

If you liked this Book Please Rate and Review!

Interested in more?
Explore the "Dfour Press" Author's Page
by Scanning the QR Code.